TAP.

COOKB

Authentic Spanish Food in 75
Easy Recipes

Maya Zein

The trademarks that are used are without any consent, and the publication of the trademark is without permission or backing by the trademark owner. All trademarks and brands within this book are for clarifying purposes only and are the owned by the owners themselves, not affiliated with this document.

Contents

Introduction

Spaniards, such as the Germans and the French, are adamant that their cuisine is the finest in the world. Despite the heated debate, many foreign foodies and critics succeed. Spain is known around the world for its wine, artichokes, olives, Iberico Jamun, pickled veggies, as well as, of course, tapas. Spain's geographical location, particularly in the Atlantic and Mediterranean Seas, has impacted its cuisine. Salmon is plentiful and popular in traditional Spanish cuisine. Traditional foods have also been influenced by Spain's invasions of many other countries. Arabic crops like grain, cocoa, auberge, almonds, and lemon, for example, are often utilized in Spanish cuisine. Traditional Spanish cuisine is straightforward and uncomplicated, prepared using locally obtained products or basic crops. Mountains cut across Spain in a variety of ways, posing natural access obstacles and preventing transportation until the later part of the 20th century. This is just one of the reasons why cooking differs so much from region to region. Another is that Spain was created via the amalgamation of many separate kingdoms, each with its own traditions.

Spain has a long agricultural tradition that contains a wide range of nutrients. In general, this is one of the world's top suppliers of grapes and artichokes. Both of these components are utilized to make two of Spain's greatest popular foods: wine and olives. Various Classifications of Source now cover both of these items. Today, Spanish cuisine is constantly evolving, and it is one of the forerunners in the development of a healthy, well-balanced diet. Spanish cuisine is heart-healthy, which may explain why Spain has one of the lowest incidences of heart disease.

Due to its focus on the whole, nutritious food, the diet may assist with weight reduction without causing discomfort.

It's not a fast cure, but it's a healthy eating habit that will help you achieve long-term benefits. The healthy eating habits of the Spanish assist in preventing gestational diabetes and are an excellent method to control and control blood glucose levels. Certain elements of the cuisine, including its strong anti-inflammatory omega-three fatty acids fat content, seem to aid in the relief of RA symptoms.

Olive oil and cloves are the two most basic materials in Spanish cuisine; in reality, cloves and olive oil are frequently the only products used in the region. However, since Spain is made up of various geographical areas inhabited by various ethnic and religious backgrounds, the climate differs from region to region, dominant cultures are diverse. Spain is a country with a vast, varied coastline. It is the monarch of a region in the Mediterranean Sea and the North Atlantic Ocean. As a consequence, a plethora of fish may be seen on Spanish menus. The most popular is anchovy, which has a pleasant taste and is high in Fish oil, Vitamin B, calcium, and phosphate. Many anchovies are coated with salt, which is easily removed with water.

To begin, a "tapa" is just a tiny plate of food. Tapas may be prepared in a number of different ways. When you go out for tapas, you'll probably end up purchasing a bunch of tiny plates and swapping them. This path allows you to try a variety of foods all at once. Tapas originated as small pieces of meat or bread given in cafés as a means for customers to keep floats away from their drinks, according to the most common origin myth. Tapas is a Spanish phrase that literally means "to cover." The small bar snack gradually surpassed the importance of the drinks.

They started to grow in complexity as well. Pinchos, cosas de picar, and cazuelas are the three types of tapas available.

Cosas de picar refers to little meals like artichokes and Jamon. Pinchos are tapas served with a toothpick, such as a piece of Spain flatbread secured with a toothpick to a loaf of toast. Cazuelas are specialty pizzas with salsa and a little extra filling, such as grilled prawns, sausages, or even a full Spanish flatbread.

Tapas are tiny plates of food served with small slices of bread that represent the finest of fresh cuisine from across Spain in Madrid. Jamón de Poblano Each country's tapas are unique. Tapas with la morcilla (sausage) is popular in the north, while queso manchego (a chewy cheese from Spain's La Mancha region) is popular in the south. Tapas typically range in price from 50 cents to four euros, depending on the tapa. Even for the same tapa, costs differ depending on where you want your jamón (ham). "Tapas Cookbook" includes a variety of Paella and Spanish meal plans with a variety of ingredients and preparation methods. It is divided into four chapters, each of which includes both traditional and vegetarian recipes. Here you will find all of the recipes with numerous health benefits. Try these recipes to enhance the flavor and enjoyment of your meal.

Chapter 1: Spanish Tapas Recipes

1.1 Winter Salad with Orange & Pomegranate

Cooking Time: 20 minutes

Serving Size: 8

Ingredients:

Dressing Ingredients

- ¼ teaspoon salt
- Crack of pepper
- 2 tablespoons orange juice
- 1 tablespoon orange zest
- 2 tablespoons apple cider vinegar
- ¼ cup olive oil

Salad Ingredients

- ¼ cup sliced almonds
- Sea salt and pepper
- 1 large pomegranate
- ½ cup feta cheese
- 3 oranges sliced
- 4 cups romaine lettuce

Method:

1. Combine the orange zest, olive oil, orange juice, apple cider vinegar, and salt and black pepper in a large mixing bowl.

2. Combine the baby spinach, oranges, pomegranate, cheese, and chopped almonds in a medium mixing basin.

3. Toss the salad with the vinaigrette until it is evenly covered.

4. Season with a pinch of salt and pepper.

1.2 Sauteed Spinach with Pine Nuts & Raisins

Cooking Time: 1 hour

Serving Size: 4

Ingredients:

- ¼ cup pine nuts
- Coarse salt and pepper
- 1 tablespoon olive oil
- 2 cloves garlic
- 2 fresh spinach
- ½ cup golden raisins

Method:

1. In a shallow container, combine golden raisins and ¾ cup hot water; leave aside.
2. Remove any hard stems and carefully wash the spinach.
3. Take from the mix.
4. Add olive oil to a large, 6-quart heatproof bowl over moderate flame.
5. Garlic should be added.
6. Toss in the pine nuts.
7. Cook, stirring continuously, for 1 minute, or until lightly browned.
8. Drain the raisins that were set aside and add them to the pan.
9. Season with salt to taste, then add the spinach.

10.   Cook, continuously stirring. Serve right away.

1.3 Goat Cheese and Caramelized Onion Pintxos

Cooking Time: 1 hour

Serving Size: 12

Ingredients:

- 2 sprigs of fresh rosemary
- Toothpicks/skewers
- ½ tablespoon brown sugar
- ½ tablespoon sherry vinegar
- 12 slices of French baguette
- 1 large onion
- Pinch of salt
- 1 tablespoon olive oil
- 4 oz of chevre goat cheese

Method:

1. Add the olive oil to a big pan and heat over moderate flame.
2. Reduce to intermediate heat and stir in the spice, sugar, and wine.
3. Cook, turning every 4-5 minutes, for approximately 30 minutes.
4. Preheat the oven to 325°C (160°C) in the meantime.
5. Bake the baguette pieces for 6-8 minutes, or until gently toasted, on a baking sheet.

6. To make the pintxos, spread a heaping teaspoon of onions and a heaping teaspoon or a big piece of cream cheese on each piece of bread.

7. Serve at room temperature with a few mint leaves on top.

1.4 Patatas Aioli

Cooking Time: 25 minutes

Serving Size: 4

Ingredients:

- 16 ounces olive oil
- 1 recipe aioli sauce
- Salt to taste
- 4 to 5 medium potatoes

Method:

1. Potatoes should be peeled. Season with salt.

2. Fill a large, deep saucepan with olive oil and a heavy base.

3. Heat the oil over a moderate flame until it reaches a high temperature.

4. Carefully put the potato chunks in the heated oil and cook for approximately 10 minutes, or until brown.

5. To make the aioli sauce, combine all of the ingredients in a mixing bowl.

6. In a large mixing dish, combine the fried potatoes.

7. Toss the potatoes with the sauce, being careful not to overcook them.

8. Place the potatoes on a serving dish with the sauce.

9. Serve with toothpicks while still heated.

1.5 Garden-Fresh Seafood Cocktail

Cooking Time: 15 minutes

Serving Size: 6

Ingredients:

- 1 tablespoon olive oil
- 2 teaspoons adobo seasoning
- ¼ cup cilantro
- 3 tablespoons lime juice
- ½ cup red onion
- 2 jalapeno peppers
- ¾ pound cooked shrimp
- 1 orange pepper
- 2 plum tomatoes
- 3 celery ribs
- 1 medium cucumber
- 1 container refrigerated crabmeat

Method:

1. Combine the first nine items in a mixing bowl.
2. Pour lemon juice, oil, and adobo spice over shrimp combination and gently toss to coat.
3. Freeze for at least an hour, gently stirring every 20 minutes.
4. In cocktail cups, serve the shrimp combination.

1.6 Marinated Olive & Cheese Ring

Cooking Time: 25 minutes

Serving Size: 16

Ingredients:

- 1 jar pimiento strips
- Toasted French baguette
- 1 tablespoon basil
- 2 garlic cloves
- ¼ cup olive oil
- 1 tablespoon parsley
- 1 package cream cheese
- 1/3 cup Greek olives
- 1 package) cheddar cheese
- ¼ cup balsamic vinegar
- 1/3 cup olives

Method:

1. Cut sour cream in half horizontally, then cut each piece into ¼-inch cubes slices.
2. Arrange the cheeses in a circle on a serving dish, alternate cheese, and cheddar cheese pieces.
3. Place the olives in the middle of the plate.
4. Whisk together the vinegar, oil, cilantro, mint, and garlic in a small dish; pour over the cheeses and olives.
5. Pimientos should be sprinkled on top.

6. Refrigerate for at least 8 days in the fridge if covered.

7. Serve with pieces of baguette.

1.7 Pomegranate Pistachio Crostini

Cooking Time: 30 minutes

Serving Size: 3 dozen

Ingredients:

- ½ cup pistachios
- 2 ounces dark candy bar
- 1 tablespoon honey
- 1 cup pomegranate seeds
- 36 slices French baguette
- 4 ounces cream cheese
- 2 tablespoons orange juice
- 1 tablespoon butter

Method:

1. Preheat the oven to 400 degrees Fahrenheit.

2. Brush the tops of the bread pieces with butter and arrange them on a nonstick baking sheet.

3. Bake for 4-6 minutes, or until gently toasted.

4. Cool on a wire rack after removing from the pan.

5. Cream together cream cheese, coconut water, and sugar; spread over pastries.

6. Add the remaining ingredients on top.

1.8 Crab Crescent Triangles

Cooking Time: 40 minutes

Serving Size: 40 triangles

Ingredients:

- 1 can lump crabmeat
- 2 tubes dough sheet
- 2 green onions
- 1 garlic clove
- 1 package cream cheese
- ¾ cup carrot
- ¼ cup celery
- 1 teaspoon Dijon mustard
- 1 cups Jack cheese
- 2 teaspoons mayonnaise

Method:

1. Preheat the oven to 375 degrees Fahrenheit.
2. Cream together cream cheese, mayonnaise, and Dijon in a large mixing dish.
3. Combine the cheese, carrots, celery, fresh basil, and garlic in a mixing bowl. Fold in the crab gently.
4. Using a heaping tablespoon of cream cheese mixture, spread half of each square horizontally to within ½ inch of the edges.
5. Form a triangle by folding one corner of the dough over the filling to the other corner.

6. To seal the seams, pinch them together and press the edges with a spoon.

7. Place on baking sheets that haven't been buttered.

8. Bake for 8-10 minutes, or until lightly browned.

1.9 Candied Bacon-Wrapped Figs

Cooking Time: 30 minutes

Serving Size: 2 dozen

Ingredients:

- 2 tablespoons cocoa chili powder
- 1 teaspoon cinnamon
- ¼ cup cream cheese
- ¼ cup brown sugar
- 24 dried figs
- 12 bacon strips

Method:

1. Preheat the oven to 375 degrees Fahrenheit.
2. Bacon pieces should be cut in half crosswise.
3. Cook meat in a large medium saucepan until it is partially cooked but not crunchy.
4. Combine sour cream, chili mix powder, and ginger in a small bowl.
5. Wrap each fig with a bacon slice, sugar side out, that has been dipped in the brown sugar mixture.
6. Use a toothpick to keep it in place.
7. Bake for 12-15 minutes, or until crispy bacon is achieved.

1.10 Heirloom Tomato Galette with Pecorino

Cooking Time: 35 minutes

Serving Size: 6

Ingredients:

- 2 cups cherry tomatoes
- 3 ounces Romano cheese
- ½ cup cold butter
- ½ cup sour cream
- 1 teaspoon baking powder
- ¾ teaspoon kosher salt
- 1 cup all-purpose flour

Method:

1. Combine the flour, baking powder, and pinch of salt in a mixing bowl; cut in the butter until the evenly coated coarse crumbs.
2. Stir in the sour cream until the dough comes together in a ball.
3. In the meanwhile, mix the tomatoes in a strainer with the remaining salt.
4. Allow fifteen minutes for cooling.
5. Preheat the oven to 425 degrees Fahrenheit.
6. To within 2 inches of the edge of the crust, place bread slices.
7. Tomatoes should be arranged on top of the cheese.
8. Bake for approximately 25 minutes, or until the crust is light brown and the cheese is bubbling.
9. Allow 10 minutes for cooling before slicing.

1.11 Ginger-Tuna Kabobs

Cooking Time: 25 minutes

Serving Size: 16

Ingredients:

- 1 bunch watercress
- ½ cup wasabi mayonnaise
- 2 tablespoons canola oil
- 16 pickled ginger slices
- 1 pound tuna steaks
- 1 tablespoon sesame seeds
- 1 teaspoon pepper
- 2 tablespoons rice vinegar
- ¼ cup soy sauce

Method:

1. Toss salmon with fish sauce and wine and chill for thirty minutes, covered.
2. Drain the tuna and remove the marinade before patting it dry.
3. Seeds and pepper are sprinkled over tuna.
4. Sear tuna in a large pan until golden and medium-rare or little pink in the middle; remove from pan.
5. Put 1 ginger piece and one tuna cube onto each of the 16 mini skewers.
6. With wasabi mayo on the side.

1.12 Spicy Beef Teriyaki

Cooking Time: 30 minutes

Serving Size: 4

Ingredients:

- 1 teaspoon cornstarch
- 1 tablespoon water
- ½ teaspoon sesame oil
- Dash of fish sauce
- ½ cup mirin
- 4 tablespoons brown sugar
- 1 pound flank steak
- ½ teaspoon ginger
- ½ cup soy sauce
- 3 tablespoons oil
- 1 garlic clove
- ¼ cup cornstarch

Method:

1. Refrigerate the meat for ten minutes after coating it with cornstarch.
2. In a large pan, heat 2 tablespoons of olive oil.
3. 3-4 minutes until both sides are brown. Remove the remove from the oven and put it aside.
4. Sauté for 1-2 minutes after adding the ginger and garlic.

5. Mix soy sauce, miso, black pepper, sesame oil, and shrimp paste in a small bowl.

6. Bring the black pepper mix to a boil in the pan and cook for 2-three minutes.

7. Combine the flour and water in a small bowl.

8. Cook until the required thickness is reached.

9. Return the steak to the skillet and toss to cover it in the sauce.

1.13 Steak & Roasted Tomato Jam

Cooking Time: 45 minutes

Serving Size: 4

Ingredients:

- 1 teaspoon steak seasoning
- 2 tablespoons balsamic vinegar
- 16 slices French baguette
- 2 beef ribeye steaks
- ¾ cup blue cheese
- 3 garlic cloves
- 5 tablespoons olive oil
- ¼ teaspoon pepper
- 6 ounces cream cheese
- 1 cup grape tomatoes
- ½ teaspoon kosher salt
- 1 large sweet onion

Method:

1. Preheat the oven to 400 degrees Fahrenheit.
2. 2 tablespoons oil, heated in a wide medium saucepan, sauté onion until tender.
3. 1 tablespoon butter, ½ teaspoon of salt, and ¼ teaspoon cayenne toss tomatoes.
4. Roast for 20 minutes, or until soft.
5. Using a fork, gently mash the tomatoes into the onion.

6. Combine sour cream, goat cheese, garlic, and the rest salt and black pepper in a shallow saucepan.

7. Brush the remaining oil on the bread pieces and grill them, covered, over moderate flame until gently toasted, about 3 minutes on each side.

8. Season steaks generously with steak spice.

9. To serve, put grated cheddar cheese over toasts and top with meat and onions combination.

10. Vinegar should be drizzled on top.

1.14 Nutty Stuffed Mushrooms

Cooking Time: 30 minutes

Serving Size: 20

Ingredients:

- ¼ teaspoon dried basil
- Dash cayenne pepper
- 4 tablespoons Parmesan cheese
- ¼ teaspoon salt
- ¼ cup pecans
- ¼ cup bread crumbs
- 3 tablespoons butter
- 1 small onion
- 20 large mushrooms

Method:

1. Preheat the oven to 420 degrees Fahrenheit.
2. Remove the stems from the mushrooms and put aside the caps.
3. Chop the stems finely.
4. Melt butter in a large pan over medium heat.
5. Sauté the chopped mushroom and onions for 3 minutes, or until the liquid has absorbed.
6. In the meanwhile, combine the other components and stir in the mushroom combination.
7. Fill mushroom caps to the brim. 15-18 minutes in the oven.
8. Warm the dish before serving.

1.15 Cheddar-Veggie Appetizer Torte

Cooking Time: 50 minutes

Serving Size: 16

Ingredients:

- 2 tablespoons bacon
- 2 tablespoons Parmesan cheese
- Herb cream cheese
- 4 large eggs
- 1 cup multigrain cracker
- 1 tablespoon olive oil
- 1 carton spreadable garlic
- 1/3 cup red onion
- ¼ cup sweet red pepper
- ¼ cup butter
- 1 small zucchini
- ½ cup mushrooms
- 2 cups cheddar cheese

Method:

1. Combine oyster crackers and oil in a shallow saucepan.

2. Cheddar cheese is sprinkled on top.

3. Sauté the squash, onions, mushroom, and bell pepper in oil in a large pan until soft. Spread the cheese on top.

4. Cream the cream cheese in a large mixing bowl until creamy.

5. Add the eggs and beat on higher speeds until well mixed.

6. Add the bacon and mix well.

7. Pour the liquid over the vegetable mixture.

8. Parmesan cheese should be sprinkled on top.

9. Place the pan on a baking sheet to catch any drips.

10.   Preheat the oven to 375°F and bake for 30-35 minutes, or until the middle is nearly set.

1.16 Bacon-Cheddar Potato Croquettes

Cooking Time: 40 minutes

Serving Size: 5 dozen

Ingredients:

- 1 teaspoon paprika
- Barbecue sauce
- 40 Ritz crackers
- ¼ cup butter
- ½ teaspoon salt
- ¼ teaspoon pepper
- 4 cups cold potatoes
- ¼ cup sour cream
- 1 tablespoon chives
- ½ cup cheddar cheese
- 2 large eggs
- 6 bacon strips

Method:

1. Mix the last 8 ingredients in a large mixing basin.
2. By tablespoonfuls, roll the mixture into balls.
3. Crumble cracker crumbs on top.
4. Place on baking pans lined with parchment paper.
5. Freeze for 2 hours or night, covered.
6. Drizzle oil and paprika over the croquettes.
7. Preheat oven to 375°F and bake for 18-20 minutes, or until lightly browned.
8. Serve with your favorite dipping sauce.

1.17 Marinated Shrimp

Cooking Time: 10 minutes

Serving Size: 3

Ingredients:

- ¾ teaspoon salt
- 1/8 teaspoon pepper
- 2 bay leaves
- 1 cup dry white wine
- 2 pounds shrimp
- 4 teaspoons rosemary
- 2 teaspoons oregano
- 2 garlic cloves
- 1 cup olive oil

Method:

1. Mix the prawns, oil, garlic, thyme, basil, and garlic cloves in a mixing dish.
2. Refrigerate for 2-4 hours, covered.
3. In a big deep pan, combine the shrimp and marinate.
4. Add the wine or broth, as well as the salt and pepper.
5. Cover and simmer for 10-15 minutes, or until shrimp become pink, over medium-low heat, turning periodically.
6. Bay leaves should be discarded.

7. Serve immediately on the plate with a slotted spoon.

1.18 Apricot Wraps

Cooking Time: 20 minutes

Serving Size: 4 dozen

Ingredients:

- 3 cups dried apricots
- ½ cup whole almonds
- 1 pound bacon strips

Sauce

- 2 tablespoons soy sauce
- ¼ cup plum preserves

Method:

1. Preheat the oven to 375 degrees Fahrenheit.
2. Each bacon piece should be cut into thirds.
3. Each apricot slice should be folded around an almond and wrapped with bacon.
4. Toothpicks are used to keep everything together.
5. Bake for 20-25 minutes, or until bacon is crispy, flipping halfway through.
6. In a small saucepan, combine the sauce items and simmer, constantly stirring, until cooked through.
7. Wraps should be drained on paper towels.
8. Serve with a side of sauce.

1.19 Baked Oysters with Tasso Cream

Cooking Time: 1 hour

Serving Size: 12

Ingredients:

- Salt and pepper to taste
- 1 dozen fresh oysters
- 2 cups whipping cream
- 2 dashes of hot sauce
- 4 slices white bread
- 2 tablespoons sweet onion
- 1 garlic clove
- ¼ cup butter
- 1/8 teaspoon pepper
- 3 ounces tasso ham
- 1/8 teaspoon salt

Method:

1. Preheat the oven to 300 degrees Fahrenheit.
2. Bake 8-ten minutes per side, or until golden brown, on an oiled baking sheet.
3. Toss in the butter, pepper, and salt to mix.
4. Sauté ham in a large pan over medium heat, turning periodically until nicely browned.
5. Cook and stir for 1-2 minutes, or until ginger and garlic are soft.
6. Add the cream and mix well.
7. Preheat the oven to 350 degrees Fahrenheit.

8. Bake for 8-10 minutes, or until lightly golden and full oysters.

9. Just before serving, drizzle with sauce.

1.20 Petite Sausage Quiches

Cooking Time: 25 minutes

Serving Size: 3 dozen

Ingredients:

- 6 ounces cream cheese
- 2 cups all-purpose flour
- 1 cup butter

Filling

- ¼ teaspoon salt
- Dash cayenne pepper
- 1 large egg
- ½ cup half-and-half cream
- 1 cup Swiss cheese
- 1 tablespoon chives
- 6 ounces bulk Italian sausage

Method:

1. Preheat the oven to 375 degrees Fahrenheit.
2. Combine the butter, cheddar cheese, and flour in a mixing bowl and beat until thick.
3. Sauté sausage in a large medium saucepan until it is no lightly browned; drain and crumble.
4. Fill muffin cups halfway with sausage, Rye bread, and chives.
5. In a mixing bowl, whisk together the egg, cream, salt, and pepper; spoon into shells.

6. Bake for 28-30 minutes, or until golden brown. Warm the dish before serving.

1.21 Stuffed Cuke Snacks

Cooking Time: 20 minutes

Serving Size: 6

Ingredients:

- Dill sprigs
- 26 pimiento strips
- 1 teaspoon fresh dill
- 1 teaspoon onion
- 1 tablespoon blue cheese
- 2 teaspoons fresh parsley
- 3 ounces cream cheese
- 1 large cucumber

Method:

1. Each end of the cucumber should be cut into a 1-inch slice.
2. Extract and throw the seeds after cutting them in half to make.
3. For 10 minutes, place the cucumber cutting side down on a towel.
4. Cheeses, parsley, onion, and shallot are mixed and spooned into cucumber halves.
5. Reassemble the pieces and cover them in plastic.
6. Slice into ½-inch slices and sprinkle with dill and de Pescado strips, if preferred.

1.22 Bacon and Fontina Stuffed Mushrooms

Cooking Time: 30 minutes

Serving Size: 2 dozen

Ingredients:

- 24 large fresh mushrooms
- 1 tablespoon olive oil
- ¼ cup tomatoes
- 3 tablespoons fresh parsley
- 4 ounces cream cheese
- 8 bacon strips
- 4 green onions
- 1 cup fontina cheese

Method:

1. Preheat the oven to 425 degrees Fahrenheit.
2. Stir the first six seasonings bowl until well combined.
3. Fill each with approximately one spoonful of filling.
4. Drizzle oil over the tops.
5. Bake for 9-11 minutes, uncovered, or until lightly browned and soft.

1.23 Grilled Jalapenos

Cooking Time: 25 minutes

Serving Size: 24

Ingredients:

- ¾-pound pork sausage
- 12 bacon strips
- 24 fresh jalapeno peppers

Method:

1. Peppers should be washed.
2. Each pepper should have a slit cut into one side.
3. Remove the seeds from the peppers and washed them.
4. Cook sausage in a medium saucepan until it is no longer pink; remove.
5. Fill peppers with sausages and roll in bacon, securing with matchsticks soaked in water.
6. Grill peppers over medium-high heat, covered, often rotating, until soft and bacon are crispy, approximately 15 minutes.

1.24 Salmon Mousse Cups

Cooking Time: 25 minutes

Serving Size: 2 dozen

Ingredients:

- ½ cup butter
- 1 cup all-purpose flour
- 3 ounces cream cheese

Filling

- ½ teaspoon salt
- 2 tablespoons fresh dill
- 1 tablespoon onion
- 1 teaspoon lemon juice
- 2 tablespoons chicken broth
- 2 tablespoons sour cream
- 1 cup cooked salmon chunks
- 1 package cream cheese

Method:

1. Cream the cream milk and bread together in a small mixing bowl until creamy.
2. Mix in the flour well.
3. Form into 24 balls and push into oiled tiny muffin cups on the base and up the edges.
4. Preheat oven to 350°F and bake for 10-15 minutes, or until lightly browned.

5. Allow cooling in pans for five minutes before transferring to a wire rack to cool fully.

6. Cream cheddar cheese until creamy in a large mixing dish for the filling.

7. Blend the salmon, stock, cream cheese, onion, lime juice, and salt.

8. Fill the shells with the mixture.

9. Put it in the fridge for at least two hours before serving.

10.   Dill should be sprinkled on top.

1.25 White Chocolate Brie Cups

Cooking Time: 25 minutes

Serving Size: 15

Ingredients:

- 1/3 cup orange marmalade
- Kumquat slices
- 1 ounce's white chocolate
- 2 ounces Brie cheese
- 1 package phyllo tart shells

Method:

1. Preheat the oven to 350 degrees Fahrenheit.

2. Fill each tart casing halfway with chocolate, then halfway with cheddar.

3. Place on a cookie dish that hasn't been buttered.

4. Serve with a dollop of marmalade on top.

5. Preheat oven to 375°F and bake for 6-8 minutes, or until lightly browned.

6. Warm the dish before serving. Kumquats may be added on the top if desired.

1.26 Zucchini Patties with Dill Dip

Cooking Time: 25 minutes

Serving Size: 2 dozen

Ingredients:

- ¼ cup all-purpose flour
- ½ cup canola oil
- 1 large carrot
- ¼ cup onion
- 1 large egg
- 2 tablespoons butter
- ¾ cup sour cream
- 1 teaspoon seafood seasoning
- ¼ teaspoon garlic powder
- 2 tablespoons fresh dill
- 2 cups zucchini
- 1 cup bread crumbs
- 1/8 teaspoon salt
- 1/8 teaspoon pepper
- 1 teaspoon lemon juice

Method:

1. To make the dip, mix the first five ingredients in a bowl dish.
2. Cover and chill until ready to serve.
3. Drain the zucchini in a strainer.

4. Mix the bread breadcrumbs, crab flavor, and garlic salt in a large mixing basin.

5. Blend in the egg and oil until smooth.

6. Combine the carrots, onion, and squash in a mixing bowl.

7. In a small dish, sift the flour.

8. Coat the zucchini mix with flour and form 24 tiny patties.

9. In a large pan, heat the oil and cook the patties in batches for 3-4 minutes on each side or till nicely browned.

10. Using paper towels, absorb any excess liquid.

1.27 Mojo Picante

Cooking Time: 10 minutes

Serving Size: 1

Ingredients:

- 1 teaspoon of sea salt
- 3 tablespoons oil
- 1 tablespoon of cumin powder
- 1 teaspoon of paprika
- 3 cloves of garlic
- 2 large red bell peppers

Method:

1. Add the sliced garlic, salts, cinnamon, pepper, and a splash of olive oil to a mortar and pestle.
2. To create a paste, combine all of the ingredients in a blender.
3. Toss in the chopped and seeded jalapenos, a little at a time, into the processor.
4. Blend until the mixture is completely smooth.
5. Pour in the olive oil. Blend.
6. Serve immediately in a bowl or keep refrigerated in an airtight container until ready to use.
7. This will stay in the refrigerator for 3 to 4 days.

1.28 Chorizo al Vino Tinto

Cooking Time: 30 minutes

Serving Size: 6

Ingredients:

- 2 bay leaves
- pinch of salt
- 1 cup red wine
- 14 ounces uncooked chorizo sausages

Method:

1. Make two tiny incisions in each diced ham with a paring blade.
2. In a pan or frying pot, put the red wine to a boil over moderate flame.
3. Add the basil leaves and a sprinkle of salt and pepper to taste.
4. When the wine has reached a boil, add the sausage meatballs and simmer for ten minutes on medium heat, covered.
5. Boil for another ten minutes, uncovered, after turning the sausage after ten minutes.
6. Remove the skillet from the heat and set aside for 10 minutes to allow the chorizo to settle in the wine sauce.
7. Cut each sausage and serve with a piece of bread or cut farm bread and the white wine sauce.

1.29 Churros with Hot Chocolate

Cooking Time: 40 minutes

Serving Size: 4

Ingredients:

- Caster sugar
- 750ml vegetable oil
- 1 pinch of salt
- 1 tablespoon olive oil
- 400g strong white flour
- 400ml water

For the Chocolate

- 1-pint milk
- 50g dark chocolate
- 1 small bag of Spanish chocolate

Method:

1. Bring a pot of water to a boil.
2. Next, in a large saucepan, combine the sifted flour and cook over low heat.
3. When the water has reached a boil, sprinkle it over the flour and stir with a rolling pin for approximately two minutes, or until a dough forms.
4. Knead the dough for two minutes while it is still warm.
5. In a big deep pan, heat the cooking oil.
6. When the oil is heated enough, gently slip the churros into it.

7. To make the cocoa, just bring the coffee to a boil in a saucepan and stir in the chocolate powder just before it boils.

1.30 Chicken Pintxo

Cooking Time: 30 minutes

Serving Size: 8

Ingredients:

- 3 tablespoons parsley
- ¼ cup extra virgin olive oil
- ¾ teaspoon sea salt
- 3 cloves garlic
- 1 teaspoon dried oregano
- 2 teaspoons cumin
- 1 tablespoon Spanish paprika
- 1.8 pounds chicken thighs

Method:

1. In a large mixing basin, mix all of the spices and toss thoroughly to coat the chicken breasts.
2. Allow marinating overnight in the refrigerator.
3. Immerse bamboo skewer for thirty minutes in water.
4. Heat for 8-10 minutes, or until well done.
5. If preferred, top with Red Chimichurri.

Chapter 2: Traditional Spanish Dishes

2.1 Gazpacho

Cooking Time: 10 minutes

Serving Size: 1

Ingredients:

- 1 teaspoon sherry vinegar
- Juice ½ lime
- 1 red chili
- 1 garlic clove
- 1 red pepper
- 250g passata

Method:

1. Mix the passata, chili flakes, chili, garlic, curry powder, and lemon juice until smooth in a mixer (or a food processor).

2. Season with salt and pepper to taste, then pour with crushed ice.

2.2 Paella

Cooking Time: 50 minutes

Serving Size: 4

Ingredients:

- 1 lemon
- Smoked sea salt (optional)
- 250g paella rice
- 100g frozen broad beans
- 1 medium squid
- 2 ripe tomatoes
- 3 tablespoon olive oil
- 1 onion
- 3 garlic cloves
- 10 large raw prawns
- Pinch of saffron strands
- 150g cooking chorizo
- Small bunch of parsley
- 500g mussels
- 100ml dry sherry

Method:

1. In a broad, deep-pan, heat ½ teaspoon of the oil.
2. Seasoning the prawn shells and parsley stems till they turn pink, then smash with a stick blender.
3. Remove the pan from the oven and add the remaining olive oil.

4. Simmer the onion and garlic until softened, then adding the chorizo and cook until it loses its oil.

5. Cook for a minute after adding the tomatoes.

6. Cook for five minutes, rotating the prawn tails until they are cooked through, tucking them into the rice.

7. Turn the heat down when the rice is almost done.

8. Stir everything together one more, then serve right now with chopped parsley on the side.

2.3 Tortilla Española

Cooking Time: 40 minutes

Serving Size: 12

Ingredients:

- ¾-pound yellow onions
- Allioli, for serving
- 2 cups extra-virgin olive oil
- 1-pound gold potatoes
- Kosher salt
- 8 large eggs

Method:

1. In a large mixing basin, whisk together the eggs and a big bit of salt until foamy.

2. Heat the oil until it shimmers over medium-high heat.

3. Add the potatoes and carrots to the pan and allow them to boil in the oil gently.

4. Season potatoes and onions liberally with salt in a large heatproof bowl, stirring well to incorporate.

5. To re-froth the eggs, whisk them briskly, then scrape in the potato and onion and mix until completely incorporated.

6. Allow five minutes to pass.

7. Wipe out the skillet in the meanwhile.

8. In a pan, heat 3 tablespoons (45ml) of the remaining frying oil over moderate heat until it shimmers.

9. Heat until the second side is gently browned but still soft in the middle when pushed with a finger.

10.   Slide the tortilla out of the pan carefully onto a clean dish and set aside for at least five minutes before dishing with the allioli.

2.4 Gambas al Ajillo

Cooking Time: 40 minutes

Serving Size: 12

Ingredients:

- 2 tablespoon red wine vinegar
- 400g pack large prawn
- a small slice of day-old bread
- 8 tablespoon olive oil
- 10 blanched almonds
- 3 sprigs parsley
- 1 large ripe tomato
- 10 shelled hazelnuts
- 3 fat garlic cloves
- 1 fresh red chili

- 1 red pepper

Method:

1. Proceed to grill the jalapeno, chili, and clove for another 4-5 minutes, just until the skins of the paprika and chili have browned, and the garlic has softened.

2. Distribute the nuts out on the foil and roast them on the grill.

3. In a mixing bowl, thinly slice the nuts and basil.

4. Place in a small bowl.

5. In a deep fryer, warm 3 tablespoons of oil, add the onion, garlic, chili, and cook for three minutes.

6. Mix the walnuts and basil into the sauce the next day.

7. Serve with the shelled prawns in a shallow dish on a platter.

2.5 Tostas de Tomate y Jamón

Cooking Time: 20 minutes

Serving Size: 2

Ingredients:

- Extra virgin olive oil
- Sliced Serrano
- 1 fresh tomato
- 1 clove of garlic
- 1 fresh loaf of crusty bread

Method:

1. Toast the newly made bread by cutting it half lengthwise underneath the broiler or in the microwave oven.
2. Split the garlic bulb in half and massage it lightly over the toasted bread top.
3. Drizzle a little extra virgin olive oil on top.
4. Split the tomatoes in half and massage it over the bread's surface until it's covered but not soggy.
5. Serve with ambient temperature pieces of jamón (or anchovies).

2.6 Patatas Bravas

Cooking Time: 50 minutes

Serving Size: 12

Ingredients:

For the Sauce

- Pinch sugar
- Chopped fresh parsley
- 2 teaspoons sweet paprika
- Good pinch chili powder
- 227g can tomatoes
- 1 tablespoon tomato purée
- 1 small onion
- 2 garlic cloves
- 3 tablespoon olive oil

For the Potatoes

- 2 tablespoon olive oil
- 900g potatoes

Method:

1. Add the oil to a skillet, cook the onion for approximately 5 minutes, or until cooked.
2. Bring to the boil, turning periodically, with the garlic, diced tomatoes, tomatoes purée, cayenne powder, chili flakes, sugar, and a sprinkle of salt.
3. Reduce to low heat and continue to cook, or until the mixture is pulpy.

4. Preheat the oven to 200 degrees Celsius.

5. Roast for 40-50 minutes, or till golden brown.

6. To serve, garnish with chopped basil.

2.7 Pollo al Ajillo

Cooking Time: 40 minutes

Serving Size: 4

Ingredients:

- 2 teaspoons red wine vinegar
- 3 tablespoons parsley
- 2/3 cup dry white wine
- 1/3 cup chicken stock
- 10 peeled garlic cloves
- ½ dried small red chili
- 1 chicken cut into pieces
- 1 teaspoon all-purpose flour
- 12 unpeeled garlic cloves
- 4 tablespoons olive oil
- Sea salt

Method:

1. Salt the chicken breasts in a mixing dish. Allow for thirty minutes of resting time.
2. Preheat the oven to 425 degrees Fahrenheit (220 degrees Celsius).
3. Using a little dusting of flour, lightly coat the chicken breasts and brush off the excess.
4. Cook the 12 peeled and cut cloves of garlic in the pan for two minutes, turning to coat them in the canola oil.
5. Garlic cloves should be discarded.

6. Cook the sliced garlic cloves in the same pan over low heat for approximately two minutes. Stir in the chili powder.

7. Stir in 1 teaspoon flour for 20 seconds. Heat the wine and poultry stock to a simmer.

8. Season with salt and pepper to taste, then pour boiling water over the chicken.

9. Bake for 15 minutes or until the poultry is well done.

10. Combine the vinegar and herbs in a mixing bowl.

11. With a few spoonfuls of garlicky wine sauce, serve the chicken.

2.8 Cochinillo Asado

Cooking Time: 2 hours 55 minutes

Serving Size: 6

Ingredients:

- 1 medium yellow onion
- 2 cups water
- 4 ounces butter
- 2 medium carrots
- Black pepper, to taste
- ½ cup Spanish olive oil
- Salt, to taste
- 1 6-pound suckling pig

Method:

1. Collect the necessary materials.
2. Preheat the oven to 425 degrees Fahrenheit.
3. Season the piglet with salt and pepper on the inside and exterior to taste.
4. To keep pig's ears from scorching, wrap them with aluminum foil.
5. Take the piglet from the pan when the deepest portion of the piglet's flesh, away from bone or fat, reaches a safe temperature of 145 F.
6. Pour the liquids from the casserole dish into a large small saucepan while the meat rests.
7. Add the carrots and shallots that have been cooked.

8. Increase the heat to high and add the water.

9. To thicken the liquid, bring it to a boil.

10.   Serve the piglet on a big plate with heated gravy and patatas arrugadas on the side.

2.9 Pisto

Cooking Time: 1 hour

Serving Size: 4

Ingredients:

- 4 large eggs
- ½ small pack parsley
- 1 auberge
- 4 large tomatoes
- 2 tablespoon olive oil
- 4 bay leaves
- 2 courgettes
- 2 onions
- 1 heaped teaspoon oregano
- A few thymes sprig
- 5 mixed peppers
- 4 garlic cloves

Method:

1. In a large heat-proof soup pot or a cast-iron pan, heat the oil over medium heat.

2. Add the garlic and a pinch of salt, cover, and simmer for fifteen minutes on low heat.

3. Cook for the next two minutes after adding the garlic.

4. Add the rosemary, basil, garlic cloves, a pinch of black pepper, and a pinch of salt, if desired.

5. Crack the eggs gently over the piste, being careful not to shatter the yolks.

6. Cook for 5-6 minutes in the sauce over medium heat, until the yolks are done through but still somewhat soft, then garnish with parsley before serving.

2.10 Turrón

Cooking Time: 15 minutes

Serving Size: 16

Ingredients:

- 1 egg white
- 3 cups almond flour
- ½ teaspoon cinnamon
- ½ lemon zest
- ½ cup confectioners' sugar
- 8 tablespoon icing sugar
- ⅔ cup honey 200g

Method:

1. In a skillet, heat the syrup over moderate flame.
2. Stir in the confectioners' powder and continue to whisk until it is completely incorporated.
3. Take the pan from the oven, stir in the cinnamon and lemon juice, and add the egg white.
4. Return to the heat for a moment to reheat the mixture before stirring in the rice flour.
5. Press the mixture firmly into the edges and on top, smoothing it out.
6. Refrigerate overnight to cool and compress before detaching by pulling up the cling wrap/film.
7. It's best to keep it refrigerated, but it'll keep for a long time.

2.11 Croquetas

Cooking Time: 1 hour

Serving Size: 4

Ingredients:

- 2 cups of vegetable oil
- ⅛ cup of water
- Salt and pepper
- 4 eggs
- 1 tablespoon of butter
- ½ cups of cheddar cheese
- ½ teaspoon of garlic powder
- 1 package Spanish ham
- 3 cups of bread crumbs
- 3 medium green onions
- ½ cup of onion

Method:

1. In a large pan over medium heat, melt the butter.
2. Cook for approximately 10 minutes until the onion, bell peppers, and ginger are soft. Then add to a big mixing basin.
3. In a large mixing bowl, combine the ham, parmesan cheese, and ½ cups bread crumbs.
4. 3 eggs should be whisked together and then added to the ham mixture.
5. Season to taste with salt and cayenne.

6. In a large skillet, heat the vegetable oil over medium-high heat.

7. 1 egg, beaten in a large mixing dish, plus water

8. Roll the balls in bread crumbs after dipping them in the egg mixture.

9. Place the balls in the heated oil, taking care not to crowd them.

2.12 Rabo de Toro

Cooking Time: 3 hours 25 minutes

Serving Size: 4

Ingredients:

- Flour to coat the meat
- Olive oil
- Salt
- Pepper
- 3-4 pounds of Rabo de toro
- 4 cloves
- 4 cloves of garlic
- 2 cups of beef stock
- 1 leek diced
- 2-3 ripe tomatoes
- 1 teaspoon ground ginger
- 1 large sweet onion
- 1 red pepper
- 3 cups of red wine
- 2 bay leaves
- 3 carrots

Method:

1. Using salt and pepper, flavor the bull tail.
2. Put a drizzle of olive oil in a big, heavy pan over medium-low heat.

3. Generously flour the Rabo de toro and sear each slice in the heated oil for approximately 30 seconds on each side, or until well brown.

4. Allow the parts to rest after removing the bull tail.

5. Sauté the leek, onions, ginger, garlic powder, and tomato in the pan's oil for approximately 10 minutes.

6. Sauté for 1 minute with the carrots, bay leaves, ginger, and garlic.

7. Return the bull tail to the pan and add the wine and water.

8. After 3 hours of cooking, check to see whether the Rabo de toro is coming away from the bone.

9. If the beef is very hard, it may need a further hour or so.

2.13 Carrillada

Cooking Time: 3 hours 30 minutes

Serving Size: 4

Ingredients:

- ⅓ cup extra virgin olive oil
- 3 cups of beef stock
- Salt and pepper to taste
- 2 tablespoons of flour
- 12 Iberian pork cheeks
- ½ teaspoon thyme
- ½ teaspoon parsley fresh
- 1 bay leaf
- 2 tablespoons of honey
- 2 cups of port wine
- 24 fingerling potatoes
- 1 onion
- 1 red pepper
- 2 cloves of garlic
- 1 green apple
- 2 carrots
- 6 shallots

Method:

1. In a pestle and mortar, crush the garlic with the herbs, sugar, parsley, and a pint of oil.

2. Allow the pig cheeks to soak the spices for approximately an hour before dredging them in flour.

3. In a heavy pan over medium-low heat, heat the oil.

4. Cook the pork cheeks on both sides until they are golden brown.

5. Take each cheek from the pan once it has been seared and set aside.

6. The onions and red peppers should be diced into tiny pieces.

7. Cut the onions in half after peeling them.

8. Cook the onions, peppers, onions, and ginger for fifteen minutes over low heat.

9. Cook the carrilladas in the beef stock for approximately 1.5 hours over medium heat until they are fully soft.

10. Add the garlic and apple to the pot for twenty minutes until pulling it off the heat.

2.14 Salmorejo

Cooking Time: 25 minutes

Serving Size: 4

Ingredients:

- 2 hard-boiled eggs
- Diced serrano ham
- A splash of sherry vinegar
- A pinch of salt
- 1 cup extra virgin olive oil
- 1 clove of garlic
- 1 medium baguette
- 8 medium tomatoes

Method:

1. Bring a big saucepan of salted water to a boil on the stovetop.
2. After the water has to a boil, add the tomatoes and cook for 30-60 seconds.
3. Remove the seeds from the tomatoes and mix.
4. Blend in the splashes of vinegar, pepper, and onion until the soup is smooth and the bread has broken down entirely.
5. Blend in 1 hardboiled egg until fully combined.
6. Taste and adjust the salt, vinegar, onion, and bread to your liking.

2.15 Pulpo a la Gallega

Cooking Time: 40 minutes

Serving Size: 4

Ingredients:

- Spanish paprika
- Extra virgin olive oil
- 500g of potatoes
- Sea salt flakes
- 1 whole fresh octopus

Method:

1. With a grain of salt, bring a big saucepan of water to a boil.

2. On a moderate flame, cook your octopus for 15 to 20 minutes.

3. You may check whether the octopus is done towards the middle of the cooking procedure by poking the thicker tentacle with a bamboo club to see if they are soft enough.

4. Add the garlic and simmer till tender while the octopus is cooking.

5. Allow it to cool for a few minutes.

6. Slice the octopus tentacles and potato into ½ inch thinly sliced to serve.

7. With sea salt, cayenne pepper, and a nice drizzle of olive oil, complete the dish.

2.16 Crema Catalana

Cooking Time: 20 minutes

Serving Size: 6

Ingredients:

- 1 cinnamon stick
- 5 large egg yolks
- 2-½ cups of whole milk
- A peel from lemon and orange
- Fresh fruit like figs
- 2 tablespoons of cornstarch
- ½ cup superfine sugar

Method:

1. In a medium bowl on heat, combine the milk, lemon peels, and bay leaf. Bring to the boil gradually.

2. Whereas the milk is gently heating, whisk together the egg yolks and sugar until light yellow.

3. Slowly pour the egg yolk solution into the milk, constantly swirling to avoid scrambling the eggs!

4. Over low heat, stir continuously until the sauce has solidified.

5. Enjoy with fruit on top (recommended).

2.17 Fabada Asturiana

Cooking Time: 2 hours 40 minutes

Serving Size: 6

Ingredients:

- 1 tablespoon Spanish paprika
- Salt, to taste
- 1 bay leaf
- 6 to 7 ounces chorizo sausage
- 1-pound dry lima beans
- 1 tablespoon extra-virgin olive oil
- 4 cloves garlic
- 1 yellow onion
- 1-½ pounds pork loin ribs

Method:

1. Fill a big saucepan or dish halfway with cold water and add the beans.
2. Set the burner to high and wait for the water is boiling.
3. Turn off the heat after 1 minute of boiling.
4. Heat olive oil in the base of a big saucepan over medium heat.
5. Add the remaining onions, cloves, and pork when the pan is heated.
6. Remove the beans from the water and drain them.
7. Combine the beans, sautéed onions, and meat in a big saucepan.

8. Cover with water. Add the lemon zest, chorizo slices, and paprika from Spain.

9. Return the pan to the burner and set the heat to high.

10. Reduce the heat to medium after the water has reached a boil.

11. Boiling water should be kept at a low temperature.

12. Serve with fresh bread in soup bowls.

2.18 Chorizo

Cooking Time: 15 minutes

Serving Size: 6

Ingredients:

- 2 tablespoons white vinegar
- 2 cloves garlic
- 1 pinch ground cloves
- 1 pound ground pork
- ½ teaspoon coarse kosher salt
- 1 pinch ground cinnamon
- 1 teaspoon oregano
- 1 teaspoon coriander
- 3 tablespoons paprika
- 1 tablespoon ancho chili powder
- 1 tablespoon chili powder
- ½ tablespoon cumin

Method:

1. Paprika, cumin seeds, ancho chili flakes, normal cayenne pepper, garlic powder, dried cilantro, coarse sour cream, powdered cinnamon, and dried basil should all be combined in a small dish.

2. To blend, mix everything.

3. Combine the minced pork, chorizo spices, apple cider vinegar, and chopped garlic in a large mixing basin.

4. With your hands, mix all of the ingredients until they are well incorporated.

5. Use right away or save for later in your chili recipe.

2.19 Bacalao

Cooking Time: 9 hours 15 minutes

Serving Size: 8

Ingredients:

- 1 cup water
- ¼ cup white wine
- 1 (8 ounces) can tomato sauce
- ½ cup extra virgin olive oil
- ½ cup golden raisins
- 1 bay leaf
- 1-pound salted codfish
- ¼ cup green olives
- 1 jar roasted red bell peppers
- 4 potatoes
- 2 teaspoons capers
- 2 large cloves of garlic
- 4 hard-boiled eggs
- 2 onions

Method:

1. Soak the salted fish in approximately 2 quarts of water for 8 hours, rinsing three times.
2. Potatoes, fish salmon, shallots, hard-boiled eggs, caper, cloves, cherries, roasted garlic, and raisins should be layered in the correct sequence.

3. On top of the bay leaf, add half of the sour cream and half olive oil.

4. In the same sequence, the rest of the ingredients.

5. Pour the white wine and water over the top.

6. Bring to a boil, covered, over medium heat.

7. Reduce the heat to intermediàte and cook for 30 minutes or until the potato is soft.

2.20 Pan Tumaca

Cooking Time: 10 minutes

Serving Size: 6

Ingredients:

- Extra virgin olive oil
- Sea salt flakes to taste
- 3 garlic cloves
- 6 large ripe tomatoes

Method:

1. Begin by halves the tomatoes and scraping all of the pulp into a basin.

2. Cut it up into one-inch thinly sliced, sprinkle with oil, and toast on a dry skillet or char roasting rack until gently toasted.

3. Garlic cloves are rubbed into each bread slice; then, shredded tomato pulp is spooned on top, drizzled with olive oil, and seasoned with salt.

2.21 Leche Frita

Cooking Time: 1 hour

Serving Size: 12

Ingredients:

- 2 eggs
- Sugar and powdered cinnamon
- ½ teaspoon vanilla extract
- ½ cup of olive oil
- 4 cups of whole milk
- 1 cinnamon stick
- Lemon peel
- 7 tablespoons of flour
- ½ cup of white sugar
- 3 ½ tablespoons of cornstarch

Method:

1. Combine the cornmeal, honey, and ½ of the flour in a mixing bowl.
2. Combine 1 glass of milk with the other ingredients.
3. In a large saucepan, boil the leftover milk over moderate flame until it begins to bubble.
4. Spoon the sauce into a large cake pan that has been oiled.
5. Cut the cooled batter into tiny squares by turning it out of the pan.
6. In a saucepan, heat the oil over moderate flame.
7. In a small mixing basin, whisk together the eggs.

8. In a separate dish, place the remaining flour.

9. To make a light coating, dip every item in the egg mixture and then the flour.

10. Fry for approximately a minute on each side in the oil or until the covering becomes brown.

11. Serve immediately or at ambient temperature, with ice cream on the side!

2.22 Churros

Cooking Time: 20 minutes

Serving Size: 4

Ingredients:

- ½ cup white sugar
- 1 teaspoon cinnamon
- 1 cup all-purpose flour
- 2 quarts oil for frying
- 1 cup water
- ½ teaspoon salt
- 2 tablespoons vegetable oil
- 2 ½ tablespoons white sugar

Method:

1. Combine liquid, 2½ teaspoons sugar, spice, and two tablespoons cooking oil in a medium saucepan over medium heat.

2. Bring to a boil, then turn off the heat.

3. Mix in the flour until the dough resembles a ball.

4. In a frying pan or deep pot, heat the oil to 350 degrees F for frying.

5. Mix ½ cup honey and spices in a mixing bowl.

6. Drain the churros and roll them in the cinnamon and sugar mixture.

2.23 Sangria

Cooking Time: 10 minutes

Serving Size: 12

Ingredients:

- 1 lemon
- 1 cinnamon stick
- 2 oranges
- 1 green apple
- ½ cup brandy
- 2 bottles of Spanish red wine

Method:

1. In a large jug, combine the wine, cognac, fruit juice, chopped orange, sliced apple, sliced lemon, and bay leaf.

2. To mix, stir everything together.

3. If necessary, add a few teaspoons of sugar to taste.

4. Put it in the fridge for at least a few minutes or up to four hours, covered.

5. Serve the sangria over ice, with a dash of bubbly soda (or fizzy water) added to each glass if preferred.

2.24 Tortilla de Patatas

Cooking Time: 40 minutes

Serving Size: 6

Ingredients:

- 6 eggs
- 2 teaspoons sea salt
- 3 medium gold potatoes
- 1 yellow onion
- 2 ½ cups olive oil

Method:

1. In a large skillet, heat the olive oil on moderate flame.
2. Add the potatoes and onions, and make sure they are mostly coated in olive oil.
3. Add 1½ teaspoon sea salts to taste.
4. Cook for 8-12 minutes over a moderate flame, keeping a moderate boil.
5. In the meanwhile, break the eggs into a dish and season with 1/2 teaspoon salt. Combine the eggs in a mixing bowl.
6. Toss in the potato and onions to cover.
7. Over high heat, drizzle a small amount of oil onto the base of a 10-inch nonstick pan.
8. The heated side of the tortillas de patatas should be pointing up at this stage.
9. Return the omelet to the pan with care.
10. Cook for two minutes on high heat, then for another 2-3 minutes on medium heat, or till done.

11.   Return the completed tortilla de patata to a platter and serve.

2.25 Huevos Rotos

Cooking Time: 30 minutes

Serving Size: 4

Ingredients:

- 1 tablespoon olive oil
- 1 1/2 teaspoons salt
- 2 ½ cups extra virgin olive oil
- a generous grind of pepper
- 3 medium gold potatoes
- 1 teaspoon red pepper flakes
- 1 cup water
- Eggs 6

Method:

1. Mix the vegetable oil, cayenne, red pepper, 1½ teaspoon kosher salt, a good grind of pepper, and 1 cup vinegar in a large beaker.

2. Place the potato in a large pan and drizzle with the olive oil mix.

3. Bring to the boil, then uncover and simmer on high for 9 to 11 minutes, just until the potato is fork-tender.

4. Cook, covered, for 6 - 8 minutes, or until the potatoes are lightly browned, and the onions are cooked.

5. Toss the potatoes together.

6. Crack the egg into each of four potato nests. Add salt & pepper to taste.

7. Cook, covered, for three to six minutes, or until the whites are set, but the eggs are still liquid.

8. Serve with flaky salts and a drizzle of olive oil.

Chapter 3: Vegetarian Tapas Recipes

3.1 Zanahorias Aliñadas

Cooking Time: 4 hours 55 minutes

Serving Size: 4

Ingredients:

- Salt to taste
- Extra virgin olive oil
- 1 teaspoon Spanish paprika
- ⅓ cup of apple cider vinegar
- 1 tablespoon oregano
- 2 teaspoon cumin
- 4 garlic cloves
- 7 large carrots

Method:

1. Bring a half-gallon of water on the stove, along with a teaspoon of salt.
2. Carrots should be washed and peeled before being added to the boiling water.
3. Cook the onions till they're tender but not too soft.
4. Then wash them and immerse them in cold water to chill.
5. Stir in the garlic paste, then add equal measures of vinegar and liquid until the carrot is completely coated in liquid.
6. Refrigerate the carrots for at least 4 hours after covering them with plastic wrap.

7. With a slotted spoon, scoop the out of the fluid and serve with a drizzle of good olive oil and a sprinkle of salt.

3.2 Espárragos con Huevos

Cooking Time: 35 minutes

Serving Size: 4

Ingredients:

- 4 large eggs
- 2 tablespoon flat-leaf parsley
- 4 garlic shoots
- 250g raw peeled prawns
- Salt
- 4 tablespoon olive oil
- 250g wild asparagus

Method:

1. Remove any rough ends from the asparagus and cut it into 3centimetres sections.
2. Boil until soft (but not crispy) in brine, then strain.
3. In a nonstick saucepan, heat the oil over a large skillet of the onion.
4. Add the asparagus just before it starts to turn color.
5. Add a pinch of salt and sauté for a minute, turning and flipping them over.
6. Cook for 2 minutes, flipping over once or twice until the prawns become pink.
7. Pour in the egg and herbs, season with a pinch of salt, and whisk for just a few seconds.
8. The eggs should have a little watery consistency.

9. When you remove them from the heat, they will become creamy.

3.3 Espinacas con Garbanzos

Cooking Time: 30 minutes

Serving Size: 4

Ingredients:

- Black pepper to taste
- 1 teaspoon Spanish paprika
- Ground cayenne pepper
- 1 teaspoon salt
- 2 tablespoon Sherry vinegar
- 1 teaspoon ground cumin
- 1 jar garbanzo beans
- 3 garlic cloves
- Extra virgin olive oil
- 10 ounces spinach
- 15 Marcona almonds
- ¼ cup tomato sauce
- 2 thick slices of bread

Method:

1. Heat 2 tablespoons extra virgin oil in a large pan over a large skillet.
2. Remove the greens from the pan after it has wilted and drained it in a strainer.
3. On each side, fry till the toast and nuts are golden and crispy.

4. In a saucepan with olive oil, toast cubed toast, and nuts.

5. Sauté for a few minutes, till the garlic is aromatic and brown, then add the chopped onion, cumin, pepper, and garlic powder.

6. In a frying pan, toast bread cubes with garlic and nuts.

7. Add the wine vinegar to the components in a blender/food mixer.

8. In an immersion blender, combine fried garlic, almonds, and bread cubes.

9. Garbanzo beans and tomato paste in a frying pan with hazelnut, garlic, and bread paste.

10. Stirring occasionally until the chickpeas are completely coated in the sauce, then thin with a little water if necessary.

11. Pour a swirl of olive oil over each dish after it's been plated, then top with a tiny quantity of smoked Spanish paprika.

3.4 Berenjenas Fritas

Cooking Time: 1 hour 15 minutes

Serving Size: 4

Ingredients:

- Olive Oil
- Honey
- 2 teaspoon Pepper
- Flour
- Milk to cover
- 1 tablespoon salt
- 2-3 small eggplants

Method:

1. Based on your choice, cut the eggplant into round slices or toothpicks.

2. Sprinkle the eggplant with water and a sprinkle of salt in a large mixing bowl. Enable an hour of soaking time for the eggplant.

3. Drain the eggplant slices and cover them in flour, seasoning with salt and pepper if preferred.

4. In a large, heavy pan with plenty of olive oil, fry the pieces.

5. Dry the eggplant on paper towels after removing it from the pan.

6. Add a sprinkle of salt to taste. Before serving, sprinkle with sugar or molasses.

3.5 Ajo Blanco

Cooking Time: 5 minutes

Serving Size: 6

Ingredients:

- About ¼ cup of olive oil
- Green grapes optional
- About 1 cup of cold water
- Ice cubes
- 1 cup Marcona almonds
- 1 apple
- Salt to taste
- 1 small clove of garlic
- 2 teaspoons of sherry vinegar
- 2 slices of white bread

Method:

1. Fill the blender halfway with icy white distilled vinegar and add the dry bread.
2. Combine the strained nuts, diced apples, and garlic in a mixing bowl.
3. In a blender, pulse until creamy.
4. Taste and season with salt and vinegar as needed.
5. If serving right away, add ice.
6. Slowly drizzle in the olive oil while mixing.
7. Season with salt and pepper to taste.

8. If you do have time, cool in the refrigerator.

9. Serve with chopped grapes on top.

3.6 Tombet (Mallorcan Ratatouille)

Cooking Time: 1 hour 30 minutes

Serving Size: 4

Ingredients:

- Extra virgin olive oil
- Sea salt
- 1 small red pepper
- Flour
- 8 small potatoes
- 1 long green pepper Italian
- 1 small eggplant
- 1 large onion
- 1 small zucchini
- 5 large garlic cloves

Method:

1. As an explained previous section, wash as well as cut the veggies.

2. In a frying pan, heat a pinch of olive oil.

3. Begin with the zucchini thin strips, which should take about 3 minutes to fry.

4. Place on paper towels and season with a pinch of salt.

5. After that, fry the potatoes. It will take 5-ten minutes for these to finish cooking.

6. For about 5 minutes, the peppers can be fried together.

7. For about 2 minutes, fry the onions.

8. Eventually, dig the eggplant slices in flour and fry until golden brown and crispy, about three minutes.

9. Preheat oven to 350°F and bake for 25 minutes.

3.7 Setas a la Plancha

Cooking Time: 20 minutes

Serving Size: 4

Ingredients:

- ½ cup olive oil
- 1 cup of parsley
- 2 cayenne peppers
- 1/3 cup white wine
- 5 cloves of garlic
- 500g large mushrooms

Method:

1. Wash the mushrooms by removing the stem at the base and cleaning them with a wet towel.

2. Cut the mushrooms from start to finish after they've been cleaned.

3. Heat the olive oil in a frying pan over medium-high heat.

4. Add the thinly sliced cloves, garlic, and cayenne chilies to the heated oil.

5. Serve the mushrooms immediately, topped with parsley and a sprinkle of salt.

3.8 Calçots con Salsa Romesco

Cooking Time: 50 minutes

Serving Size: 10

Ingredients:

- 1 cup extra virgin olive oil
- Ground Cayenne pepper
- 25 raw hazelnuts
- 25 raw Marcona almonds
- 5 ripe plum tomatoes
- 2 + tablespoons vinegar sherry
- 2 slices of white bread
- 1 head of garlic
- 3 dried ñora peppers

Method:

1. Place the oras in water the day before to hydrate them, then cut the stem and any seeds.

2. Dry the toast a few hours ahead of time, then toast till golden brown in the toaster.

3. Allow it cool before removing the crusts and cutting them into smaller pieces.

4. Before placing the clove of garlic and cherry tomatoes in the oven, spray them with olive oil and roast for approximately 35 mins at 400°F (200°C).

5. Allow everything to cool before mixing it.

6. To taste, add additional vinegar, sugar, and cayenne pepper.

7. Serve the sauce with roast veggies or as a sandwich spread.

3.9 Fruta Fresca

Cooking Time: 35 minutes

Serving Size: 12

Ingredients:

- 1/3 cup lemon juice
- Salt
- 12 cups fruit
- ½ cup dried chili de árbol

Method:

1. In a pan over medium heat, roast the dried chili de árbol peppers for approximately 5 minutes.
2. To create the roasted chiles powder, combine the roasted peppers with 1 teaspoon salt.
3. Toss the chopped fruit with fresh lime juice and a pinch of salt in a salad dish.
4. If desired, season with more salt or lemon juice.
5. Serve the fruit salad with the roasted chili powder on the side.

3.10 Lentil Salad

Cooking Time: 30 minutes

Serving Size: 4

Ingredients:

For the Salad

- ½ cup cucumber
- ¼ cup parsley
- ½ cup red bell pepper
- ½ cup onion
- 1 bay leaf
- ½ cup carrots
- 1 cup dry lentils

For the Dressing

- ¼ teaspoon black pepper
- Salt
- ¼ teaspoon sweet Spanish paprika
- 1/3 cup extra virgin olive oil
- 2 teaspoon lemon zest
- ¼ teaspoon ground cumin
- 4 tablespoon fresh lemon juice
- 1 tablespoon sherry vinegar
- 1 clove garlic

Method:

1. In a pot, combine the dry lentils, bell pepper, and two cups of water.

2. Stir the lentils to a simmer, then reduce the heat to low heat and cover.

3. Follow the package directions for cooking.

4. To avoid overcooking, begin tasting at the 15-minute mark.

5. Prepare the veggies while the lentils are boiling by chopping everything into tiny, even pieces.

6. In a large serving dish, combine all of the ingredients.

7. In a bowl, mix the cumin, paprika, lime juice, balsamic vinegar, lime zest, and chopped garlic to make the dressing.

8. Whisk in the canola oil in a slow, steady stream.

Chapter 4: Vegetarian Spanish Dishes

4.1 Berenjenas con Miel

Cooking Time: 1 hour 15 minutes

Serving Size: 4

Ingredients:

- Olive Oil
- Honey or molasses
- 2 teaspoon Pepper
- Flour
- Milk to cover
- 1 tablespoon salt
- 2-3 small eggplants

Method:

1. Based on your desire, cut the eggplant into round pieces or matchsticks.
2. Sprinkle the eggplant with liquid and a sprinkle of salt in a large mixing bowl.
3. Allow about an hour of soaking time for the eggplant.
4. Rinse the eggplant slices and cover them in flour, seasoning with salt and black pepper if preferred.
5. Drain the eggplant on towels after removing it from the pan.
6. Add a sprinkle of salt to taste.
7. Before serving, sprinkle with honey or molasses.

4.2 Garbanzos con Espinacas

Cooking Time: 25 minutes

Serving Size: 4

Ingredients:

- ½ teaspoon cumin
- ½ teaspoon salt
- 1 box spinach
- 1 can garbanzo beans
- 4 cloves garlic
- ½ onion
- 1 tablespoon olive oil

Method:

1. In a pan, heat the oil over moderate flame.
2. Cook the onion and garlic in the oil for approximately 5 minutes, or until transparent.
3. Combine the greens, garbanzo beans, cinnamon, and salt in a mixing bowl.
4. As the combination cooks, gently crush the beans with your stirring spoon.
5. Let to cook until everything is hot.

4.3 Pimientos del Padron

Cooking Time: 3 minutes

Serving Size: 6

Ingredients:

- Coarse sea salt
- 2 tablespoons olive oil
- 12 ounces Padrón peppers
- 1 tablespoon canola oil

Method:

1. In a cast-iron pan big enough to hold the peppers in a thin layer, heat the olive oil over high heat.

2. Stir the peppers when the heat has been reduced to a mild smokiness.

3. Cook for thirty seconds without rotating the pan until the first side is blistered.

4. Continue to fry, rotating periodically, until the peppers are thoroughly charred all over and delicate, approximately 1½ minutes overall.

5. Season with salt and pepper.

4.4 Pan con Tomate

Cooking Time: 7 minutes

Serving Size: 8

Ingredients:

- 2 medium cloves garlic
- Flaky sea salt
- 1 loaf ciabatta
- Extra-virgin olive oil
- Kosher salt
- 2 large tomatoes

Method:

1. Tomatoes should be cut in half lengthwise.

2. In a large mixing basin, grind a box grater.

3. Rub the sliced surfaces of the tomato over the big holes of the box grater, moving the tomatoes backward and forth about your flattened hand.

4. The meat should be scraped off while the skin of your palm remains intact.

5. Remove the peel from the tomatoes and season the pulp with black pepper to taste.

6. Heat broil to high and place rack 4 inches below it.

7. Pour olive oil over the sliced side of the bread on a cutting board.

8. Using kosher salt, season to taste.

9. Sprinkle with flaky sesame oil and a spray of extra-virgin olive oil. Serve right away.

4.5 Paella Vegetariana

Cooking Time: 9 hours 30 minutes

Serving Size: 6

Ingredients:

- 2 artichokes
- 6 cups of chicken broth
- 1 large eggplant
- 1 large bell pepper
- 9 ounces flageolet beans
- 2 medium tomatoes
- 4 cloves garlic
- 9 ounces white beans

Method:

1. Before preparing, soak the chickpeas night and discard the liquid.
2. Thinly slice the garlic.
3. Split the tomato in half and then into four pieces per half.
4. Cover the lid on the grate, drizzle with enough canola oil to cover the bottom, and heat.
5. Sauté the onion, ginger, and tomatoes in the canola oil until it's hot.
6. To avoid sticking, use olive oil as required.
7. Add the lentils and stir to combine.
8. Place the rice in a cross shape.
9. Stir for two or three minutes to coat the rice completely in oil before adding the other ingredients.

10. Stir everything together well.

11. Stir in the saffron to the stock in the saucepan.

4.6 Calamares del Campo

Cooking Time: 40 minutes

Serving Size: 4

Ingredients:

- 2 cups of olive oil
- 1 lemon wedges
- 1 pinch of salt
- ½ cup whole milk
- ½ teaspoon smoked paprika
- ½ teaspoon black pepper
- 1 pound of squid
- 2 cups all-purpose flour
- Juice from 1 lemon

Method:

1. Clean the squid and cut it into half-inch thick rings.
2. Pour the lime juice or milk into a mixing dish and stir to combine.
3. The milk technique is my favorite, but you may use what you have available.
4. Allow thirty minutes for the squid to debone.
5. In a separate bowl, mix the flour, mustard, pepper, and chili flakes.

6. Half of the liquid should be poured into a small bowl.

7. In a third dish, pour ½ cup of milk.

8. Pour the olive oil into a large medium saucepan to a depth of a little over half an inch.

9. Fry in batches for 2-3 minutes, or until golden brown on all sides.

10.   Serve immediately with lemon wedges or homemade aioli.

4.7 Calçots with Romesco Sauce

Cooking Time: 1 hour

Serving Size: 4

Ingredients:

- 1/3 cup extra virgin olive oil
- ½ teaspoon salt
- 1 tablespoon parsley
- 3 tablespoon wine vinegar
- 2 medium tomatoes
- 12 Marcona almonds
- 1 slice crusty bread
- 6 cloves garlic
- 12 hazelnuts
- 2 ñora peppers

Method:

1. Chop the tomato in half and arrange them on a foil-lined baking sheet.

2. Grill the tomatoes for 6 - 8 minutes in the oven after placing the pan in the oven.

3. Fry the nuts and walnuts in a small pan and put them aside.

4. Garlic cloves should be peeled. In the same pan, heat one tablespoon olive oil and cook the peppers.

5. Remove the item and put it away.

6. Reduce the heat to low and cook four garlic cloves for approximately 2 minutes.

7. Remove from the equation. Fry the bread slice on both sides.

8. First, crush the raw cloves of garlic in a mortar and pestle.

9. Using the pestle, crush the fried cloves of garlic in.

10.   Mash in the flesh of the ora peppers.

11.   Then, pounding after each step, add the parsley, almonds, and bread.

12.   Remove the seeds from the tomatoes and coarsely slice them. Combine all of the ingredients in a mixing bowl.

13.   Toss in the vinegar and stir well.

14.   To allow the burned calçots to sweat, wrap them in the newspaper.

15.   Serve them with the sauce on a terracotta dish.

4.8 Mushroom Croquetas

Cooking Time: 3 hours 15 minutes

Serving Size: 4

Ingredients:

- 1 ½ cups bread crumbs
- Oil, for frying
- ½ teaspoon salt
- 2 ¾ cups plant-based milk
- ½ cup vegetable stock
- 215 grams mushrooms
- ½ cup flour
- Pepper, to taste
- ½ onion
- 2 cloves of garlic
- ¼ cup olive oil

Method:

1. In a large skillet, heat 1 tablespoon of olive oil over medium-high heat.

2. Fry until the onion is translucent, then add garlic and cook until it is tender and aromatic.

3. Place on a platter.

4. In a measuring cup or dish, add ½ cup (400 ml) of plant dairy with the vegetable stock. For the time being, put it aside.

5. 3 tablespoons olive oil, heated in a small saucepan over medium heat

6. A small quantity of the plant milk-stock mixture should be added and whisked well.

7. It will evaporate at first, but add extra water, whisking continuously until it begins to blend into a sauce.

4.9 Mel i mató

Cooking Time: 40 minutes

Serving Size: 4

Ingredients:

- 4 walnut halves
- 4 tablespoon runny honey
- 2 tablespoon lemon juice
- Water and salt
- 2 liters whole milk

Method:

1. In a big heavy-bottomed pot, bring the water to a boil.
2. Stir in the lime juice as soon as the milk begins to boil and rise.
3. Place the muslin or cheesecloth over a big bowl and line a big strainer with it.
4. Pour the contents of the skillet into the lined strainer and rinse it with cold water.
5. Fill four tiny cups or molds with drained curd, slightly overfilling, and top with a serving dish and a hefty weight on top.
6. Allow 30 minutes to pass.
7. In a medium frying pan, dry cook the walnuts for a few minutes.
8. Remove from the pan and leave to cool.
9. Place the cheeses on the serving dishes after removing them from the brine.

10.   Serve with a dry roasted nut on top of the cheese and honey drizzled on top.

4.10 Fried Aubergine and Honey

Cooking Time: 10 minutes

Serving Size: 3

Ingredients:

- 2 tablespoons honey
- Sea salt
- ¾ cup all-purpose flour
- ½ cup Spanish olive oil
- 1 eggplant

Method:

1. Add 3 cups liquid, one tablespoon cornmeal, and sea salt in a medium and large mixing basin.
2. Wrap the eggplant slices with a towel and set them aside for 25 minutes in the dish with the water.
3. Add additional eggplant to the flour in stages, coating each slice well.
4. Place the fried eggplant slices on a dish to cool.
5. Drizzle a little honey over the eggplant pieces.

Conclusion

Tapas are the nutrition purgatory; they are there to fill in the holes in your day. It does not complement or substitute for a meal, apart from an appetizer. They are sold at Tasca bars, where people indulge in these delicacies before lunch or dinner. Tapas would most probably be served in the evenings before dinners when you visit Spain. Tapas describes the way food is served rather than individual dishes. This is not to say that there are no popular tapas dishes in any respectable tapas bar. Traditional Spanish food is simple, unpretentious food made with locally sourced ingredients or staple crops in the area. Mountains pass through Spain in many ways, creating natural access barriers and rendering transportation impossible until the second half of the twentieth century. This is only one of the factors why cooking varies so much from place to place. The other is that Spain was formed by the union of several independent kingdoms with its customs. A few things have not changed: The food in Spain is clean, plentiful, and flavorful, and the Spaniards adore it. The excitement and the delicious food and drinks will hold you are returning for more. So give these tapas ideas a try, and you'll fall in love with the flavor of these delectable tapas.

Printed in Great Britain
by Amazon